REFLECTIONS OF A

Rose

TIFFANY ROSE

ISBN 979-8-89112-621-3 (Paperback)
ISBN 979-8-89309-374-2 (Hardcover)
ISBN 979-8-89112-622-0 (Digital)

Covenant Books
11661 Hwy 707
Murrells Inlet, SC 29576
www.covenantbooks.com

Preface

As I sit here thinking about how to begin this story, I am grateful for what I am learning in this process. Looking back on that day when my heart broke, I still feel that great hurt. It hurts so much to hear a child, my child, declare I am an unstable mother and an unreliable, unpredictable person. In my heart, I know that God sees the motives of each of our hearts and knows all truth. This story is about the reflection I have been doing about my life and where I am today as a result of some of my choices in this journey. I asked myself, "How did it come to this point? Why did it get to this?" I was recently reminded of why hardships come along in our lives and where we go from them.

> That the trial of your faith, being more precious than of gold that perisheth, though it be tried with fire, might be found unto praise and honour and glory at the appearing of Jesus Christ. (1 Peter 1:7)

I learned that the key to facing such hard times is knowing who I am in Jesus Christ.

I have been asked what made me decide to write a book. My life hasn't been easy, yet the journey I have walked has allowed me to become empathetic with others and even sometimes to help others in the midst of their journey. I am a blessed person today due in part to the things I have overcome, triumphed over, or simply been carried through them. My faith in God, my higher Source of strength and power, is what helps me to climb these mountains. It's hard to see the mountain tops when you're in the lowest valley, yet there is only one way to go now—*up*! It is then that you can reach up and take hold of the rope being held by God's hands.

I will lift up mine eyes from whence cometh
my help. (Psalm 121:1)

I was asked about the title *Reflections of a Rose.* I will try to explain what I felt that God was showing me when He planted this thought within my heart. You see plants in general need water, sunlight, carbon dioxide, and soil to grow. Roses are known for their beauty as well as their fragrances, yet most will have prickly thorns. My life at times felt beautiful, yet the *thorns* or circumstances that would come along would cause me hurt and pain. It is through that pain that God would reveal His beauty surrounding my life.

Each plant starts as a seed or embryo, and that seed within me is called faith. It is the beginning of growth, a place where plants begin. That is exactly how my faith as a child began to develop and grow. For plants to begin to grow, they need good soils, and for me, that was the foundation of faith my grandmothers would demonstrate to me. Next, a plant needs water and sunshine. In my life, the water was often my tears while God's love would become my sunshine. Just as we need oxygen to breathe, plants need carbon dioxide that we exhale. God would often breathe fresh air back into my brokenness so that I could continue to develop and grow. The plant's root system is its anchor in the soil to allow it to stand firm and tall, and in my life, that root system became my relationship with Jesus Christ. If I kept in tune with what Jesus was providing, I found I was more able to stand up.

A plant's stem begins to form from the roots and grows to allow the leaves to form and grow which allows for fruit to grow. As I grew stronger in my walk with Jesus, I began to see other relationships develop along the way that would begin a new leaf growing in my life. The stem has the job of supporting the flowers or the fruit as well as holding up its leaves toward the sunlight. It is also the transportation system for the plant's food, water, and nutrients from within the roots. I began to see how important it would become to develop that strong stem so it could withstand those circumstances in my journey. The flowers and fruit are the products of what a plant grows, so as I began to grow, I soon discovered areas where Jesus was giving me fruit or His beautiful flowers. The root in a plant is its vital link between the plant, water, and nutrients. So it would become in my life, I had to learn just how valuable the faith I had would become in my journey.

When I think of a rose, the first thing that comes to mind is its thorns. The rose itself appears beautiful in color with a wonderful alluring fragrance. To me, those thorns represent the struggles in my life along my journey, the so-called *bumps in the road*. Yes, if you prick your finger on the thorns, it does hurt and often bleeds. Yet if I look beyond these thorns, I can see a beautiful flower at the top. It can be an awesome deep red to a brilliant yellow to a soft peach tone. Its fragrance draws me closer. It is in that moment I think about the prick on my finger from the thorns and yet simply savor the moment as I breathe in the aroma and forever capture the beauty of the brilliant yellow rose.

It is my hope that in these writings and stories, you can find your beauty in your rose, knowing that the thorns along the way only point up to the beauty at the top of the stem filled with its fragrant aroma.

> I am the vine, ye are the branches: He that abideth in me, and I in Him, the same bringeth forth much fruit: for without me ye can do nothing. (John 15:5)

The Rose
Author Unknown

It's only a tiny rosebud…a flower of God's design
But I cannot unfold the petals within these clumsy hands of mine.
The secret of unfolding flowers is not known to such as I…
The flowers God opens so sweetly in my hands would fade and die.
If I cannot unfold a rosebud this flower of God's design,
Then how can I think I have the wisdom to unfold this life of mine?
So I'll trust Him for His leading each, moment of every day,
And I'll look to Him for guidance each step of the way.
For the pathway that lies before me,
My heavenly Father knows…
I'll trust Him to unfold the moments,
Just as He unfolds the rose.

Introduction

I was born on a small country farm in a rural area of Michigan. The farm was 120 acres of God's awesome beauty yet in need of living to be done. It was a family farm shared with my parents and grandparents and was in our family for over one hundred years. Originally, it was a part of a four-corner town that consisted of just a few buildings. Typical farms with chickens, cows, and yes, even a dog. The house was a typical farmhouse with a woodstove in the basement for heat. There were times we had to shovel coal for the fire or throw wood in the stove to keep its fire burning. This was my home. As farming often goes, summers meant that hay and straw had to be cut and baled then put up in the barn so it left little time for a vacation.

I was the oldest of what would become ten children with two dying shortly after their birth, yet it was a simple life back then. Dad was a foundry worker and often drove the truck while Mom was often either working at a local drugstore or bakery.

In the sixth grade, I had the opportunity to experience being in a one-room country schoolhouse next to our farm. The memories of that school resonate with me. We had a big roaster that we would bring our TV dinners to school and use to heat them up. The older kids were assigned the duties of helping out, especially with the younger students. It was at kindergarten through eighth grade. Our classes were small yet we had so much fun learning. We did Christmas plays, and I remember one year when we had a mouse deciding to join our program by running up the tree as students were performing a play. We loved our recess time and enjoyed such games as red rover or playing softball out in the field.

In May 1975, I graduated from high school and went on to college in a small town nearby. I left college in January 1977 and took a job at the local bakery. In June 1977, I took a job at a local medical care facility as a nurse's aide. It is there while caring for one of my patients I would meet my future husband. We got married in 1978, would go on to have four children, and be together for twenty years before divorce would happen. That wasn't easy for any of our family, least of all, our three children. Our eldest son had died in childbirth. The three were now in their teenage years, which came with its own struggles as well.

Later on, in 2001, I would marry a man I had befriended at our Christian Singles Dance. We would start out happy, yet with time, it also ended in divorce in 2012.

In 2014, I began to discover how lonely life can become when there isn't anyone to share it with daily. It was then I really learned just how much faith would mean to me.

I am a grandmother of nine grandchildren now. I became a Christian at eight years old while attending a revival meeting with my grandparents. I love to write and share my thoughts as God brings them to me. It is my hope that you can also find joy as you read these words. I love the mountains, and many of these words have been written during my time living out in Wyoming. While I am divorced, I still struggle at times with being alone, yet God says He will be there for me. I love to quilt when I have the time, and I love music. Because of my dear grandmother, I learned to play the piano as well as the organ. I grew up in the church that I eventually took on playing piano for too.

I love to go out in the woods for walks or along the beaches as I see God's beauty surrounding me. His nature was often my go-to when life became hard to understand.

I praise the Lord for His goodness to me, especially for His unconditional love for me. As I begin this journey of writing, I want to remember my friend Sherry who was such an example to me of trusting in Jesus. Her parting words spoken in her memory at her funeral were, "Live a life for Jesus Christ." I also want to thank my adopted mother, Gayle, for her support in all the times I needed a friend to simply listen. I want to thank God for the lessons I have learned in being a mother to my three children. It is my desire that as you read these words, you too can find common chords and my love for Jesus. Just as a rose may have thorns, it can also bear single or double flowers. I pray this may be true of these writings—you find beauty. I love Jesus Christ and praise Him for His gift of creativity within me and pray this will become a blessing to each of you as well.

Finding Strength

On October 4, 1979, labor began. I called the doctor and went to the hospital. I had seen the doctor on Monday, and he had had a difficult time getting the baby's heartbeat. After some time, the doctor was able to find the heartbeat and figured it was just the way the baby was lying on his belly. So they sent us home with an appointment to come back within a week unless labor began. On Tuesday and Wednesday, contractions were on and off, but nothing was regular. They would intensify and then stop. On Thursday morning, the contractions began, so I once again called the doctor and was told to come to the hospital. We arrived shortly after noon. A nurse checked us in. The contractions continued, but I noticed the nurses and doctors having trouble getting our baby's heartbeat. Immediately, they took me down to X-ray to get a picture of what might be happening. At 4:00 p.m., the doctor came into my room, saying, "Your baby has passed away, and you are going to have to go through a natural delivery to deliver him as we can't do a C-section." Contractions worsened, and there was more back pain as they continued throughout the night.

On Friday morning, the doctor came in and said they could break the water to hurry along the delivery. So I was taken down into a birthing room where the doctor began to help deliver our son. I had my husband at my head, a nurse pushing down on my abdomen, and the doctor working from the other end to help deliver the baby. The pain was unbearable, to say the least. Soon, our son was born. My husband assisted the nurse in cleaning him up, and then he held our son. The nurse asked me if I wanted to hold my son. I told her no, I couldn't. She suggested that I at least look at him before he was taken away. I took a quick glance at my son. (In hindsight, I wished so many times I had held him in my arms because I couldn't remember anything about him, and my husband had to tell me about our son.)

I blamed myself for our son's death. I felt I must have done something to cause his passing. One thing I recalled the nurse telling me was that he had a family trait: a certain toe was formed a certain way, and this had passed along in several generations of my husband's family. I often mourned our son and spent many times crying over his death. It took many years before I could come to the place where I forgave myself for his death or for not holding him. It took me even longer to accept the fact that I had not caused his death. You see, before I knew I was pregnant, I had been drinking an awful lot and figured this had caused his death. It was later that I discovered that he had the cord wrapped around his neck, and had God allowed him to survive, he probably would have been mentally challenged. God loved him even more and needed to call him home.

At our son's memorial, the pastor spoke of God needing a rose for His garden, and He chose our son that day as His rose of great beauty. At the time of his birth, the doctor informed me that the likelihood of having other children would be very small, if at all, because of the complications within my pregnancy and then his death. God once again proved Himself faithful to His promises and granted me three more special blessings—our children.

I mourned my son for a very long time, and every October 5, I recall that day. Seven years after our son's death, my dear grandmother on my father's side fell into my arms and went on to heaven, on October 4, 1986. I am sure that our son was one of those who greeted my grandmother at the gate of heaven. I still sometimes struggle when those first few days of October come rolling around, yet I am blessed knowing there is more than just sadness and death, as one day, I will see them both again. Six months after my grandmother passed away, her husband of sixty years was also called home to Jesus in March 1987. Grandpa said it was just too hard to go on without his love of sixty-three years. They had lost a son in a motor-cycle accident when he was nineteen years old, and Grandma had lost a daughter in her seventh month of pregnancy.

Several years later, I lost my grandmother (on my mother's side) as she succumbed to her battle with Alzheimer's disease. As her memory left her, she could only recall me as her *piano girl*.

Survival

It was tough being twelve years old and trying to figure out how to survive an experience 'I couldn't talk to anyone about. Parents were too busy to hear me; grandparents—I didn't know how to tell; pastor—I didn't feel I could talk to. In the next few years, I ran and hid whenever he came around. I took off to walk in the woods; I wrote in a journal, trying to find a way to cope. My only hope, a friend I trusted, up and moved away. I had no one I felt I could confide in.

One day, sitting in the back of my closet holding a piece of broken glass, all I thought about was wanting to kill my pain. I would get reprimanded for running away to hide when he came in the yard, yet I listened as stories were told about other parents and their daughters in similar situations. How could these other parents let their daughters spend so much time at this person's place? And overnight? So I figured out I had the solution: cut my wrists. Yet the angels of God had another plan from God Himself. I heard, "Don't do it. It is *not* the way!" I began to cry and sat there in the dark wondering, *Why can't I just end this?* This was in 1991. Many years later, I would be sitting at that same man's bedside in the hospital, telling him how much God loved him before he passed away.

In June 1975, I had my first real job outside of the farm and one day found myself in a situation with no apparent way out. I endured the pain and shame of rape. Because I hadn't found anyone to tell about the previous sexual abuse, I still didn't have anyone to turn to. My solution? Run away! So in the middle of the night, I packed my bags, stole my parents' car, and ran away. Three days later, I went to my grandmother's home to meet up with my parents. They accused me of lying, called me a whore, and kicked me out of their home. My grandparents took me in and put together a small living space in their basement for me to live in with them. I was given a place to call home again.

Grandma told my father, "She is still flesh of your flesh, blood of your blood, and if you don't want her, we will take her." My grandmother didn't know the reason I left was because of rape. I had hoped to tell her one day what she and Grandpa had done for me, yet that opportunity didn't come before she died in my arms. She took that time to teach me the art of sewing and making quilts as we talked of faith in God. At one point, Grandma stated she wanted to die at home, and if I was there when it was her time to go, she asked me not to do CPR but to let her go to Jesus. I honored her wish that day when she finally passed in my arms on October 4, 1986.

Later in my life, around the late 1990s and in my marriage, I learned how to survive again. I made the mistake of seeking love in someone else's arms, which only created anger, guilt, hurt, and pain within my marriage. It became physical, and my children and I kept uprooting ourselves repeatedly over the next five or six years until I had enough, and we divorced in 1996.

The divorce left my children with many scars and hurts that lasted a very long time. It cost me my sobriety at one point. I was becoming what I had often said I wouldn't: an alcoholic. My mother's father, my grandfather, was an alcoholic and struggled with it most of his life. I swore to myself I wouldn't do that to my family, yet I did. Thankfully, one day someone asked me what I would do if, while I was passed out drunk and my home caught fire, who would rescue my children? It was a sobering moment, and I decided to quit. I remained sober for ten years before I relapsed because my family had been invited to my former husband's wedding, and I was excluded from my own family who were attending his wedding. So I turned to the bottle to drown my pain and hurt. I started over the very next day, embarking on a new journey of recovery from alcohol.

It has been a long journey, and I have struggled along the way, but I know I have other ways to survive.

My faith is a significant source of strength in this journey.

> I will lift up mine eyes unto the hills from
> whence cometh my help. (Psalm 121:1)

Change

Webster's definition of *change* is "to make different in some particular way; to replace; to exchange for a comparable item; to put fresh covering on; syn: modify, vary, or transform." I felt this could describe my life. As a young teenage girl, I dreamed of college, marriage, and a family. It was the usual dream of most teenage girls then: to get married. Well, I have learned that dreams do change over time as well.

As I thought about changed lives, I began to recall the story of Saul in the Bible. Saul had a history of persecuting Christians but would one day become one who would be persecuted for Jesus Christ. Saul met God on his way to Damascus, and his life was radically changed. He modified his life from that of the persecutor to becoming an example of the persecuted for Jesus Christ. God gave him the name Paul, and from that point on, his life changed. After his conversion, we find that Paul went into the wilderness for a time of solitude (Galatians 1:16–17). He used this time in prayer and listening to God. He used this time to equip himself for what would become his lifetime of service. Paul acknowledged how, through his blindness, he recognized God preparing him for his future work. Paul's name means "little," which some felt was in reference to him being small in stature and his physical weakness. God can transform weaknesses into strengths.

My life, at this point, could relate to his example in many ways. I was on a road that I felt was a good one to be traveling on. Then changes began: divorce after twenty years of marriage, a dream now changing. I wasn't the perfect wife, and I admit I made many mistakes along the way. Now as a divorcee, I had to learn to modify my life from that of being a *couple* to that of being *single*. It wasn't an easy change at all. God knew I needed some time to prepare myself for my future, as Paul had done.

I sought the Lord for guidance on how to face this new challenge of starting over at forty-two years old. I felt a new road was coming ahead. I started studying the purposes behind name changes in the Bible. I also began to look into the legal issues of changing one's name. I left it to the Lord to guide me in this direction. God gave me three confirmations once a name was chosen. I chose my first name because it meant "refreshing as streams of water in the desert" (Isaiah 35:1–6). I felt like I was in a desert at this point in my life. I was now on the road to starting over anew. God was that water, the living water, which became my source of strength in everyday living. I went through the formal channels to verify my identity before legally changing my name. I went before a judge to complete the process in July 1999. It was a part of the life-changing process that God was now taking me through. I sought God's will for my life. I had a new road to travel on, a new dream. As we obey God's will, others will see the changes as they occur in our lives. God had begun the transformation as I sought His will.

Change is never easy! It doesn't happen overnight, and it cannot be done alone. I thank God He has been there, encouraging me each step of this journey. God promises His transforming presence by way of the Holy Spirit to give us both hope and help us make the changes needed to conform to His will. God's power for renewing and changing begins on the inside and works toward the outside. I learned that my struggles and trials could refine and purify me, making me stronger. When one believes in God and the restoration He offers through His Son, Jesus Christ, He turns our sinful lives into an exchange for forgiveness from God.

Even today, I am still a work in progress. I want others around me to see Jesus and my love for Him. Oh, I am not perfect by any means, and I fail Him often, but praise God for His grace and mercy.

Change is *never* easy. I change what I am able to and accept God's timing and His will for those things I cannot change on my own. I am learning that sharing, a changed life can give *hope* to others. As I share and listen to others, I hear them talk about their struggles with changes from familiar roads each has also traveled. I try to let changes make me more like Jesus, and so today, I again give praise to God for those changes He has brought me through because He truly knows what is best for me, and He knows the bigger picture!

Letting Go

Letting go is not an easy thing for anyone to do, yet sometimes it is necessary. I found I kept repeating the same patterns when it came to relationships. I would want to feel loved and needed so badly that I'd attract people into my life who needed to be *cared for*. Yet I would find myself feeling like I was simply being taken advantage of.

I recall that as far back as I can remember, I just wanted to feel I was loved for who I was, not for what I could do for someone else. Being the eldest of ten children, I was often left to do extra chores or watch younger siblings. My parents were hard workers, yet I don't recall a lot of "I love you" being said. I was often found somewhere by myself, sitting alone or being off on a walk in the woods. Even in school, I recall being a loner with not many friends. I was often considered *quiet and shy*. I didn't date much in high school as I was required to be at home to help with the chores on the farm.

I remember in sixth grade going to the little one-room schoolhouse. I found what I thought would become my one true love. Then about that time, I had hope one day that I would have a future, but that changed as one day after school, his family just up and moved away without any warning. I was heartbroken. For many years, I tried to find out where my one true love had gone. Many more years went by; we did find each other via social media and soon discovered that at different points in our lives, we had been trying to find each other. He holds a special place in my heart despite each of us taking different paths.

Love is something I struggle with in my life as a result of my journey. I was shown what love should become in the lives of my grandparents, yet I found it very hard to attain or hold on to in my journey. When I dated, I would hear, "I love you," but would soon realize it was simply words to get a physical response. It was like that in high school, again in college, and then again when I met my first husband. He was quiet and wanted to get married before he turned thirty years old. He was several years older than me, yet he told me he loved me. Yes, and for a while, I believed we had love between us. As time went on, we grew apart due to my indiscretion which resulted in our divorce. We remarried, but that marriage also ended in divorce. I was left feeling even more unloved.

About three years after that divorce, I was drawn to a man I had met at our Christian Singles event. He treated me like I was a queen, and before long, he was telling me, "I love you." I loved looking into his eyes and seeing his smile back at me. Over time, that smile turned into sadness when I looked at him. Then came a divorce. We tried once more to make our marriage work in a remarriage, yet it also failed. I truly believed it was going to work this time, but it carried the same issues as in the first marriage, and we hadn't resolved any of those issues. I began to think I would grow old with him and spend the rest of our lives together, yet it was just another dream that soon fell away. I started to feel more like his *caregiver* than his wife. It wasn't long before he stopped saying the words I so longed to hear, "I love you." I came to a decision one day that I found difficult to make; I wanted to stop the hurt and pain within my heart. I had been given a choice that was just too hard to choose. I had given twenty years into my first marriage and then another ten-plus in the last marriage. I began to grieve them both over the next several years, as I had grown up being taught that marriage was until death separated us. In a way, it was like the death of my hopes and dreams.

In July 2014, my children's father passed away suddenly and unexpectedly from colon cancer, leaving an emptiness within our family. My children didn't understand the void it left in my heart. I was driving along an expressway when I received a text, "Dad is gone." I pulled my car over to the side of that road and just wept for several minutes. He was the father of our children, my first husband before he would become their daddy, yet I had to hear of his passing via a text. In time, I had to release that hurt and let it go. They will never know how great the heartache was when he passed away. While he and I had our moments—ups and downs, good and bad times—we shared twenty years together. We did share a love once upon a time.

In 2012, my last marriage ended with divorce, and I grieved again in a different fashion. I truly believed in the beginning that he was my soulmate, as he seemed so easy to talk with. Soon, I began to see *red flags* that started giving me concerns, and I simply overlooked those things. I didn't want to settle just because I didn't want to be alone again.

Loving others means I have to first love the person I am because if I can't love the woman in the mirror, how can I expect to love anyone else?

It is still a process, even now. Letting go is never easy—yet it was what I needed to do for my own emotional well-being. I couldn't settle for just *taking care of* someone when I was feeling empty inside of myself.

33 1/2 Hours

It was a Tuesday evening in August 1996, at eleven o'clock, when she was asked to shut her light off and get to bed. "Okay, Mom, I love you." At one o'clock, my listening ears heard her footsteps go past my room to the bathroom. I listened to be sure my baby went back into her room so I could go back to sleep. As a mom, I need to know all my children are safe and sleeping before my eyes close.

Wednesday morning at eight, I heard an awful pounding at my door and the doorbell ringing nonstop. I went to the door to find a young girl in tears crying, "She's gone." I went to my daughter's bedroom to find a neatly straightened room with a note on her bed telling me she was gone.

"Please don't worry and don't cry. I love you." I began crying nonstop as my little girl was gone, and I didn't know where to look. I called 911 and cried out to them about my missing daughter. I began calling anyone who might have known where she was. I cried out to my Jesus to watch over her. Proverbs 3:5–6 reads,

> Trust in the Lord with all thine heart and
> lean not unto thine understanding, in all thy
> ways acknowledge Him and He shall direct thy
> path.

The hours seemed to drag on, and I couldn't seem to leave the telephone, hoping each time it rang I would hear my daughter say,

"Mom, it's me, and I want to come home." We followed all leads while the neighborhood and town were checked again. More calls were made, but still no word. We had been told she was on her way out of the area to meet friends and then on to Caseville. From there, on to other places, none of which were good. Friends called to pray with me, comb the town, and just be near to me and her brother. They hugged and cried with me, and we had a circle of prayer over my daughter. I had to believe that He would watch over His child. I held on to my faith and claimed the Scriptures. "The Lord is my Shepherd" kept coming to me, along with the passage that He would lead me through the valley of the shadow of death. The not knowing was my shadow of death. I had to trust and believe that God would carry me through this valley and care for my daughter as well. My friends and family from afar continued in prayer throughout the night hours.

Then came the dawn. More phone calls, more questions, and still no answers, no leads. God was still in control of everything. Meanwhile, unbeknownst to us, my daughter was preparing to come back home. We had prayed for the Lord to bind Satan and his wrong influences from my daughter. She had tried to make phone calls to reach her contact to leave the area, but the phone wasn't working right. Praise the Lord! We knew who stopped the phone from working—God Almighty!

On Wednesday at eleven o'clock, my son and I were preparing to drive into town to make flyers to fax to various people to help find our daughter. Guess what happened next? As we were driving up our road, our dear friend Sonya stopped us alongside the road and told us she had someone for us to see. What a sight to see! It was my daughter, his sister! I jumped out of my van and ran to her. I placed my arms around her and cried tears of joy, for this, my prodigal child, had been returned to me. For the next half hour, I cried and just held her tight. My first thoughts were, *Thank You, Jesus*! I was thankful God had returned her to me and had worked it all out for her to be found at just the same time Sonya was driving into town. My daughter had gone to use one phone and found it being used, so she proceeded to the next phone, where she was found. Throughout the thirty-three hours of her being missing, God kept reminding me to "be strong in the Lord and in the power of His might" (Ephesians 6:10), as found in the New Testament. I knew His arms were around me. I could feel Him holding me up when I felt I couldn't get through the hour.

My daughter was missing for thirty-three hours, and I held her tight for the first half hour after she had been returned to me. God is so good! While as a mother I wanted to do all I could to find her, it was the Lord who was in control and took care of my daughter. I praise His dear name because He is so good and heard one mother's prayer on behalf of her lost child. I know there were times when I wanted to try and fix it myself, but God held me up. He assured me that in trusting Him and in His Word, He would answer the prayers for my daughter. While we have many things to talk about, my dear daughter is safe and back home again. I cannot say enough about how good God is! My God is an awesome God! He does walk with us in the valleys as well as on the mountaintops. God is worthy of this mother's praise! I thank my Jesus for guiding her back home.

My daughter left with her plan, yet God had an even bigger plan for her. She was planning to join a gang she had met members of while on a vacation with her father. Originally there were five girls planning to run away. Three changed their minds; one left but got scared and went home. My daughter had walked about two miles and decided she was going to come back home but was afraid she was locked out of her home. As she started back, two men saw her walking and grabbed her. She was held in a local motel with them until she found the opportunity to get away to the payphone across the way. It was then that Sonya would be driving into town. We did press charges against these men, and threats were made against my daughter to harm her, so we were advised to leave the area for her safety. Once again, God was already working, as my ex-husband and I decided to try putting the marriage back together, so we moved back into his home. God is always looking out for His best for us, yet we might not see it at the time.

(The significance in thirty-three and a half? Jesus's approximate amount of time from crucifixion until His resurrection.)

You Were Created for Love

In October 1996, I attended a conference at the Judson Baptist Church in Flint called "You Were Created for Love" with Jack Frost. I went with the intention of gleaning something from the four days of the conference that would enhance my service to God. Little did I realize what God was preparing me for in those days.

Jack talked about seeing God as a loving daddy, not an angry one. Many of us thought God was an angry God because He hated sin, and we, His children, do sin. Through the meetings, I began to see God as my heavenly Daddy. He was showing more of Himself through His healing process. Jack and his wife Trisha testified of their years of marital and family problems along with *burnout*. They became aware of their need for a deeper intimacy with the Father's healing love. They showed how intimacy is really "into me see." I began to see myself and my struggle from deep within to feel loved. God revealed to me that buried deep was a lot of pain, abandonment, and rejection since birth. God needed to rid that in order to fill me even deeper with His love.

Many times, I felt like an orphan even though I had siblings in my birth family. I felt I'd been rejected since birth because I was *unplanned*, *unexpected*, and *untimely*. As I grew older, I felt I couldn't gain acceptance or approval no matter how good I was. Secretly, I longed for someone simply to love *me*!

During the meetings, as Jack spoke about those who felt like orphans, he read the Scripture from Acts 17:22–29. It speaks about how we are God's offspring (verse 29) and that He created us. In verse 26, it tells how God determined the times set for His people and the exact places for them. God chose the exact moment of my birth and the place where I would be born as well. I was God's choice…He chose me… Out of His love…I was born.

> Before I formed you in the womb, I knew you. Before you were born I set you apart; I appointed you as a prophet to the nations. (Jeremiah 1:5)

God was there at the point of my conception. I wasn't unwanted, unplanned, or an orphan because my heavenly Father designed me from the beginning to be loved and give out His love. Sometimes, it is hard for me to understand why God chose the parents we grew up with. The parents we grew up with were not the parents God intended for us because God Almighty did not create our parents *wounded*. He created our parents to be a gift of love to the world. Because of the sins of our forefathers, our parents were hurt and wounded. Hurt and wounded parents pass their hurts down to their children. Hurting people hurt people. God, my heavenly Daddy, wanted me to see that I was created in love, through love, and for love. I was created as a gift of love to the world. Loved people love people.

As my tears began to flow, a friend held me in her arms, and I just wept and wept. I couldn't stop because my "Daddy," God, was revealing to me just how much I was truly loved and wanted by Almighty God. The years of hurt, buried so deep within my heart, were being set free and being replaced with the Father's love. I began to feel love in a way that I never had known. To me, love was something I couldn't feel for a long time. I had been married for years, and while I felt I had loved my spouse, I began to realize just how little I really knew about love. Now I began to feel love in a new way…God's love…unconditional. It was a gift of love. I realize now that my family is hurting and need to be set free as I did. They were wounded people by the generations before them. Jack helped us to see how God's love was misrepresented to us. We need to change those things in our families and show the Father's love. My desire and prayer is that my family will also see the truth that they are a gift of love, created with and through love right from the moment of their conception.

You Are Loved

Finally my brother be strong in the Lord
and in the power of His might. (Ephesians 6:10)

I had been claiming this verse for about a month until Friday, August 16, 1996, when I experienced the true power of the Lord.

It started with a simple invitation to attend a spirit of renewal at Judson Baptist Church in Flint, Michigan. Little did I know just what the Lord had planned for me that night.

We began the service with praise and worship, then a time of testimony, then unto a time of exhortation, time for praying for an impartation of the Holy Spirit. My friend had been praying for me.

I felt afraid, yet God kept telling me, "Trust in me and be not afraid." He said, "It's okay, and I won't let anything happen to you."

I began praying for the Holy Spirit to come fill me. I slowly began to move one chair away from my seat toward the aisle, and then I moved two seats closer to the aisle. Soon I found I was in the middle of the aisle looking toward the altar. As I walked up toward the altar, I continued to pray. I noticed a woman come up to pray with me. She began saying, "Come, Holy Spirit. Come and fill her." I began to feel a warmth I had never known before, and I fell backward toward my friend Chuck and then down on the floor.

As I lay on the floor, I saw black clouds over me, and each one had a name. One was Darkness, another was Fear, and another was Worry. They began to part. God's words, "Be not afraid," were com-

"

forting me. God's hands were holding a rope that He reached inside me and began pulling out. Each time He'd reach inside of me, He'd pull out some of this rope with a box attached to it.

Over to my left was a sea named Forgetfulness. He would take each of these boxes attached to this rope and try to throw them away. I would grab the rope and pull it back toward me. This tug-of-war continued for quite some time. With each thing He would pull out of the depth of me, I would pull it back. These boxes were named Acceptance, Pride, Worry, Guilt, Failure, Trust, and a box named Abuse. This battle continued. I kept trying to get up, yet I could feel God's hands on my shoulders holding me down on that floor. Then I began to run away. God took hold of me and said, "I love you, Donna. I love you, and you are My child! I won't let you go. It's okay. I love you!" He held me tight. I began to cry. I knew in the very depth of me, I was *loved*. God had filled me with His peace and love. I felt warmth flowing from my toes to my head. Then I saw each of these boxes, with each of their names, fall into the sea and begin to sink. My hands were no longer holding onto the rope and neither were God's hands. I watched as each of these sank to the depths of the sea.

I looked up and saw a brilliant blue above me. It then parted to a sky of bright yellow sunshine. As I woke, I felt I had been in a major surgery. I was told by those praying over me that they could see that I had a struggle happening, so they began praying for God's peace to help me resolve that struggle. Another prayed for the Holy Spirit to fill me from the tips of my toes to the top of my head. Those who were praying over me told me I was on the floor for at least an hour and twenty minutes. I tried to lift my head but was unable, so I just laid there a little longer and enjoyed the presence of the Holy Spirit in that place. I saw men given a spirit of laughter, some unable to walk. I witnessed the spirit of joy in a young man that night. He was leaping and running with joy in that place. I knew I was in the presence of a mighty God! I *knew* the Holy Spirit was in that place! As I sat there, a verse came to me: "A friend lying down his life" (John 15:13), and I thought of what my friend had done for me, praying for me and inviting me there to that service. He knew I desired to really know the Holy Spirit and to experience His power. When I left, I felt I was walking in the clouds.

God has shown Himself more real to me. I thought I knew all I needed about the filling of the Holy Spirit. That night I witnessed and felt the real, true power of the Holy Spirit. God has told me that He isn't finished with me yet. He has more to do with me. I have only begun to walk in the water of His love. It is my desire that each of you reading this will step out into the water of God's great love. God is real, He is alive, and God loves each of you.

> Peace I leave with you, my peace I give unto you: not as the world giveth, give I unto you. Let not your heart be troubled, neither let it be afraid. (John 14:27)

Surgery Day

January 27, 1999

It was 8:20 a.m. when the telephone rang. The hospital asked if I could come as soon as possible because the doctor's schedule had changed. I said yes, I could be there in about forty-five minutes. Pat, the nurse on the phone, said to come as quickly as I could but not to put myself in danger driving there. My stomach tensed up at this point. I got my daughter up, and we were on our way momentarily. My friend met me there as my daughter left. We went to patient surgery where they expected me. We were then directed back to admitting since I would be staying in their beautiful accommodations for a few days. After admitting, we went back to patient surgery. Once in patient surgery, I quickly changed clothes, they checked my vital signs, popped in an IV, and rolled me in the stretcher. I was off to the infamous ride down to the basement, better known as *the holding tank* of the operating room. My friend prayed for me before the descent to the lower level, and the prayers were greatly appreciated. We said our "I love you" and "See you soon." Off to their holding room I went, placed in the corner staring at the picture of flowers on the wall. The nurse came into the room to give me *the pep talk* and to honor me with the ever-so-popular *surgical hat*. Oh, green wasn't my color! The anesthesiologist came in, asking his list of questions. Soon the nurse returned with her razor in hand. It was time for a quick shave! Haha! The beginning of something new—shaving my abdomen?

Next came the shot to make me drowsy, but I didn't get sleepy. Soon the nurse reappeared, saying, "There's a man waiting to see you."

I asked, "What does he look like?" which brought a chuckle from the nurse. So I was whisked from my corner and wheeled out to greet this man—my pastor. We chatted for a few minutes, and he prayed with me over the surgery. I returned to the holding area, but as the nurse rolled me away, I heard the pastor say, "Make sure she gets a driving license to operate that cart." Haha!

Back in the corner, wonderful words of praise began to fill my heart and soul. God was so good to me.

Then came the doors of the operating room. Oh, they might not have seen Him, but my God was right there the entire time, holding my hand, telling me, "It's okay. I am here for you."

God is there even in the midst of scary situations. He never leaves me or you alone.

This was once again a journey of faith together—my Lord and me!

Oh, by the way, I came through the surgery just fine. I knew God wasn't finished with me yet.

After a few days in the hospital's accommodations, I was out the door. I was slightly worse for wear but truly more blessed having been with the Lord once more.

Superbowl

January 31, 1999

I *let go* of all that *could have been* to my soon-to-be former spouse. I had gone through my surgery without him and was okay. I didn't need a spouse anymore. In his own words, "You're too old to change." I prayed he would get right with God before it's too late. That was the get-well part.

I gave glory to Jesus Christ for my life. I thanked Him for my salvation and those trials that had helped me grow stronger.

I had read about taking a helium balloon, tying a note to it, and on that note, writing down what I was feeling. I needed to release and let go of those feelings. That day had become the day to let go! At 11:55 a.m., I released my balloon from the patio door and watched as it went up in a northwest direction where I believed God was watching and waiting to grab it. I felt as if His hands were there as the balloon continued to rise toward the heavens. While I watched it rise out of sight, I thanked God for the very presence of His love for me. On another note, my friend had also released her balloon from her home, but her balloon got entangled in a tree. She said God had a further reach to grab hers, but she knew God was taking her balloon, and she was releasing and letting go of her hurt as well that day!

Second-Floor Courtroom

March 8, 1999

You sat there in the hallway as I approached. I held my head up high as I walked by. This wasn't what I had wanted. My dream had been to simply be your wife and our children's mother.

Then entered the attorney for the counter-defendant. It was time for regrouping and a pep *talk*. Off to the cubby hole we went for last-minute preparations. Back to the infamous *courtroom*. Oops! I forgot something—there was no John Hancock on the paperwork. I followed the leader back into the cubby hole. One last detail and off to the courtroom to await the verdict. I would be the third one on the court docket…but oh no…where was the plaintiff? So off to the hallway went the attorney in search of his client. Announcing the third one on the docket… "Do you solemnly swear?

"Yes, I do…"

Subject to the approval of the friend of the court, divorce would be granted. Verdict? Final *divorce*. Divorce papers were written and signed with love—and pain—endorsed with tears, and sealed with sadness.

I was now pronounced "Miss"…from a "Mrs." to miss management in sudden singleness. I praised the Lord that while I preferred the "Mrs." degree, I found strength in Him daily to keep on this road He had allowed me to travel.

Hurry, off to the hallway he went where the mistress awaited the plaintiff. The elevator doors closed as they held hands together.

Oh, the show in that moment—oh Lord, many would say I should have turned red in anger—but not with you, Lord, in my corner. I walked with my head held up high. Free—I was free—no longer under bondage. Walking down the stairs and out to the sidewalk, I knew—I truly was more blessed to have walked another mile in my journey with my Lord.

Once upon a Wife

March 17, 1999

Twenty years ago, I walked down that church aisle with so many anticipations and so much excitement. I felt as if I was walking on clouds at that moment—I was going to become your wife. Nothing could have brought me more joy. The Lord had sent wind and sun to let me know He was there with us that day too. Little did I realize how much I would come to rely on Him even more in those twenty years. God is faithful to His promises.

> I will never leave you nor forsake you.
> (Deuteronomy 31:8)

A Day's Walk

March 23, 1999

At 3:20 p.m., the telephone rang. "Hey, Mom, the car has over-heated and died. Can you find a way home?"

So I set off to walk home four miles. "Oh, surely you aren't going to walk all the way home?"

It was like what Psalty sings about—simply trusting God for the first step to climb the mountain. So it was me and God, taking that first step out the door, across the street, and heading north. Water bottle, coat, and purse in hand, away I went. Hi ho, hi ho. "Hey, thanks for the breeze, trucker!" I put one foot in front of the other. I was climbing my mountain (or hill) one step at a time. I had wanted to start walking because I wanted to—not out of necessity. "Lord, I need Your strength up this mountain." Yay, one mile down, three more to go. "Lord, I'm thankful it's not too cold or snowing."

> I lift up my eyes unto the hills from whence
> cometh my help. (Psalms 121:1)

Thank You, Lord, two miles were done! I was halfway there. God was so good to me. The birds were singing as well. "Oh Lord, I refuse to complain. Grant me strength in these legs of mine to climb this hill." I refused to let old Satan win this battle. Three miles down and one more to go. Slightly slower, but still one foot in front of the other. I was climbing my mountain (hill) all the way. It was time to switch arms—coat, purse, and water bottle—and onward we went—it was you and me, Lord. When I got to the end of the way, there would be someone to say, "Good job!" Hurrah! I reached the road—four miles finished! Thank You, Jesus. No worse for wear! Such fellowship, you and *me*. I made it!

Oh, there were those who would say I was silly to walk four miles home, but I didn't believe it. You see, it was worth the time spent with You, oh Lord, climbing that mountain called No Way Home—No Transportation. We made it, and I wouldn't take anything for that journey. Just one more in our journey together—You and *me*.

You see, trials are only opportunities to see God's faithfulness at work.

Sunday Morning

March 28, 1999

"Hey, you got tee peed last night!" What more did I need? It wasn't enough; now I saw their handiwork blowing in my trees. Then I was reminded—as it blew, I saw You there, Lord. You were in that breeze, telling me, "It is okay. I am here. I see your tears. Keep your eyes on me." Oh, they meant it as a joke, but I saw it as a blessing once more. It was a visual for all to see when it blew in the wind— just who it was in the wind—Lord God Almighty is His name!

Some mom surely was missing a lot of toilet paper!

Thank you, Father, for one more reminder along this journey of faith that you were here with me, giving me peace and strength to continue on.

Flight of New Beginning

April 29, 1999

Boarding for flight 417 began. Here I went, row 13 F, a window seat by the wing. The captain's light came on. "Fasten your seat belt." The stewardess began the safety speech. Oxygen would be available if needed. I checked out the nearest exits out of the plane in case of an emergency. Oh, Lord, it was taxiing time; we were number 12 in line to go up, up, and away. It was about 9:45 a.m., and we started to take off. Oh, perfect love casteth out all fears. Was I afraid? No, not with God as my pilot and navigator. A slight air pressure change led to an earache, and then I chewed and chewed that gum.

I couldn't forget the single men the devil sent in rows 13 D and E. They were players alright! What an awesome sight as we went up and away, thirty-three thousand feet in the air. Your beauty is so awesome; words cannot speak enough about them.

There was some turbulence along the way but nothing major with the Lord at my side. "We will be landing in twenty minutes. Fasten your seat belts."

Memories? 14 F won a free cruise. 12 E and F, Tom's proposal to Mary—she said *yes!* And he slipped the ring on her finger.

What a journey, You and me, Lord, closer to your heavens. It was truly amazing seeing such beauty—clouds that looked like whipped cream rolling across the skies. They looked good enough to eat. People said I was crazy flying so far alone. Yet they didn't know the pilot of my life, Lord.

I am truly in awe of where I am today…because of You!

Cruising Along

April 29, 1999

Those three days of rest and relaxing, Lord, I needed that—R and R. Your creation is so vast. A beautiful ocean and I was just learning to lean on you even more. Father, what valuable lessons You teach me every day. I praise You, Jesus.

Was that Your ship? The *Seabreeze*—eight hundred passengers. Had I ever been on a ship before? "Oh, you'll enjoy it. You alone? Oh, you will meet new friends." There, embarkation. Picture time. And on to Cabin E-41 (Electra deck). Wow! It was so amazing. At 7:00 p.m., the horns sounded, and we were off. Oh, we couldn't forget the 4:30 p.m. lifeboat drill. Seven short blasts and one long blast—Station 11 Muster Station D-Carmon Lounge. We passed inspection. I didn't have a buckle to hook up mine, so it was just a handy-dandy knot for now. I guessed it would do for now. Oh, the slightly rocky motion, and I guessed it was Dramamine time. So long, Fort Lauderdale and Cozumel. Two days at sea. Dancing, praising, eating, praying, rocking, swaying, and on I went. "Hello, my name is… I am from… Glad to meet you too."

Oh, Lord, I was so grateful I had You here with me—the great navigator of the seas in my life.

Max Lucado's video hit home about how the Father's heart is toward the hurts of His children. Lord, I am sorry my earthly father wasn't that for me, or our children's father's heart wasn't toward their hurts. Praise you, Jesus. You were there for all of my hurts.

Pictures with the captain? Oh, such a long line. I would wait to have my place in heaven next to my heavenly captain. What a sight that would be! Everyone was so formally dressed for the captain of the ship. If only we truly were more concerned with the hearts of our family and where they would spend eternity.

A little rocking and swaying over the ocean seas. I praised you as you were the rock that didn't roll in my life. Lord, so many claim to be Christians, but only You know the heart. It seems like just a label sometimes.

Excursion

It was Tuesday, May 4, 1999, and at 6:45 a.m., I was ready to head out for the jeep tropical safari. Cozumel, here we come! At 8:15, I headed down to G deck to the gangway. "Watch your heads and steps." Down the sidewalk with the guide in the lead, we followed the leader to the jeep safari. Teal green…four passengers, and we followed the caravan through town.

Such poverty here, Father. How I appreciated my circumstances. My life wasn't easy compared to those of Your creation. I don't live in a shack…I don't depend on tourists' tips. I am truly blessed and take many things for granted.

The top was down, the wind was blowing, and it was 80 degrees. The scenery was beautiful. "See the iguana on the left…the trail is over there…hold onto your hats…" Now it was shake, rattle, and roll time. Palm trees, sand, ocean, critters, cactus, and bumps. Oh, the bumps! Time to put it into a four-wheel drive. "Keep it in first gear in the sand so you don't get stuck." We struggled through with a good driver behind the wheel, and it was over the trail. On to the Mayan ruins to face the east. What a sight! And oh, such history here! Their belief in the goddess of love that kept their people free from crime, etc.

Truly, I am blessed to have been there where so many of your creations have gone before me. Oh, I was shaken, rocked, rattled, and sunburned but ever so mindful of just how good you are to me, Father. My life has had its bumps, and rocky roads, left in ruins, with the beauty intermingled in between it all—your beauty, your grace, your love, and your mercy. I praise You, Father, for where my life has come from and where it is going.

You alone are the one true navigator of my life. You know the way to lead me and how to bring me back around when I get stuck in the sand or hit too many rocks in the road. You keep me on the narrow road so I can stay in focus. No side trails, no detours—just straight ahead with you, Jesus.

Truly, it was a beautiful day, walking in the streets of your beautiful Cozumel. Oh, I couldn't forget the reach out and touch my children. It was so good to hear their voices. Lord, I know you'll watch over them too. They truly are a part of you. You lent them to me, and my heart goes out to them too.

All aboard! Time to prepare for Honduras, and I was ready to see what you had in store for me at this next port in my life. I knew that with you, I would go on from this stop in my life. This was not the final place. I was still moving on with you, and I was not afraid. Humanly, I longed for companionship, but you know my heart. You know I wanted to be loved again once more. You alone can provide that for me as I sailed alone, guided by You, Jesus.

Letter from "No Name"

I received a very touching letter enclosed with the thank-you note from her funeral (my mother-in-law). I was told I had shown little or no love for my husband and had given him only hurt. I was told I should have talked to my daughter about the proper funeral attire. What—black dresses weren't it? You see, the letter came in reply to one I sent "the family" in response to their lack of concern for our hurting children, who sat amidst the funeral with their mother sitting alone at the back of the church while their father sat with his mistress with "the family." The preacher announced the children and their spouses, but when it came to *my* husband, it was simply his name and his mistress's name. Ouch! That was a low blow to their honor.

I sent a letter in response to this action, which caused the said "no name" letter to be graciously presented to me via the postal service. Oh Lord, You know who was bold and who was the coward. I signed my name; "the family" did not. I was called a liar and was told that my husband was better off. Well, I guess they know more than me, and I had spent the last twenty years of my life living with him.

Father, I praise you for giving me the courage to walk into the church with my head held high—*unashamed*! One more blessing for me along this path!

Marriage License

March 31, 1999

While reading the newspaper, what should I see? Under the title of marriage licenses? My husband's name with the name of his mistress! "Do you have anything to prevent you from legally obtaining this marriage license?"

"Oh no. Oops—I forgot I do have a slight problem—my current wife! Haha! Just a slight hitch in the road."

"Two scheduled dates, but no divorce finalized, so I guess we bump your wedding back. Thirty days' expiration—no divorce—and no remarriage!"

Lord, I praise You that You created laughter for our souls. Who else would know I'd be reading the marriage license of my current husband?

Oh, I was just the first wife who became the ex-wife who then remarried him to become the second wife, only to be divorcing him to become an ex-wife again. God, You see the humor amid these tears. I praise You for the growth I made here today.

From tears to cheers, from first to ex to second to ex, and on this journey with You, as my heavenly Husband. Pruned away from the root to begin a fresh regrowth. Thank You, Jesus.

First Date Postdivorce

"Would you like to go out for dinner and a movie?"

"Sure…when? Where?"

"Mom, your date is here."

I grabbed my breath and threw off the nervousness, and off I went.

"I'll have the… Mmmm, that sounds good… Thanks. Pass the salt, please. Hey, there's the boss checking me out. Oh no, what will they think?"

It was cold and windy…sitting in a car…doors locked? I didn't want to become a crime statistic. Well, uh? Quiet conversation seasoned with the raindrops from heaven, then it was popcorn and movie time.

"Let's see, which one shall we see?"

"Hey, the kids say this one is good."

Mom all cuddled up in her movie chair in hopes that laughter would soon be there. Instead, it was sleep in the theater chair, sleep in silence sprinkled with an occasional noise. Ninety minutes later, the movie was over, and off to the taxi for the ride home.

"Oh, don't get me wrong—I enjoyed the date but realized it wasn't my scene—not just yet."

Father, You know me inside and out. I praise you that You have watched me since I was just a wee little sprout. I could make a date anytime, anywhere. I can speak or I can be silent, and I know you know my thoughts and motives. I can have candlelit dinners, and You'd always be that special guest—my date! I love You, Jesus.

Righteous Refuge

Let righteous take refuge in Him.

—Psalm 64:10

On February 2, 1999, at 1:30 p.m., a phone call was made to seek information on an upcoming court case. I became angry to discover it was being dismissed due to the lack of follow-through by the police agency with subpoenas.

I cried out to God for the rest of the day, "Lord, this isn't right. I stood up for the right. I obeyed man's laws—now it's for nothing? There will be no consequences? Your children will have seen another example of how to manipulate the judicial system."

My heart was broken and crushed. How could this be? What purpose was to be served if evil triumphed? "Lord, please let not my enemies triumph over me." He kept telling me to remember,

Vengeance is mine… Stay focused on ME!
(Deuteronomy 32:35)

New Year's Eve

On January 4, 2000, the end of a decade, the century, the millennium, time passed by so quickly. It seemed like just yesterday I was a little girl, then married, divorced, and single again.

Should old acquaintance be forgotten? Some, yes—some absolutely *not*! The house had been swept, dusted, picked up, touched up, and whipped into order for the Singles event—our New Year's gathering. Food, fun, fellowship, and looking back as well as ahead. Twist it, pull it, ha ha! Skip-Bo, Crazy, "YMCA," "Rock Around the Clock Tonight," ham roll-ups, puppy chow, 7 Up cranberry apple juice, and oh, we forgot—laughter, laughter, and more laughter!

Devil, you can't win in the end. You twist the truth, pull the lies, bop me when I'm down, and laugh at me. You lure me away from my Lord and cause me to skip the gathering of fellow saints. Some might say that I'm crazy for feeling this way. Well, let them because I'm crazy for the love of my Jesus. He is my YMCA: Yahweh-Messiah-Counselor-Almighty.

You are with me second by second, minute by minute, hour by hour, both day in and day out. You are my source of nutrients.

Laughter of the Holy Spirit takes first place there as a Merry Heart maketh glad. (Proverbs 15:13)

As I look back, I have come through, or gone around, detours in my life. You have brought me through valleys and carried me to the mountaintops. A day with you is as a thousand, so I shall not fear what lies ahead (2 Peter 3:8). Perfect love casts out fear (1 John 4:18). God's love is perfect. I might have lost some things in the past, but I've gained much more on this journey of faith. I look to the New Year, knowing you are there in all that comes my way. Oh, I might not have been hugged or kissed to usher in the New Year, new decade, or new century, but beginning with the presence of my heavenly Father in my life is worth so much more.

Thank You for the blessing of Your love and laughter!

Off the Road Again

At 5:45 a.m., the alarm went off, and it was time to rise and shine, baby. Oh, just five more minutes or so. By 6:00 a.m., I had to get up and prepare for work. I was off and running to the personally refreshing, temperature-regulated *waterfall*—the shower. Oh, it felt so refreshing! Then came the time to shiver and shake as I prepared to dress. I'd better speed up as time was beating me in this race. I blew my hair, scrubbed those pearly whites, painted my face, and slapped in the plasticware called contacts. I didn't forget that special shirt just so I wouldn't forget where I was going. All set to go and slap those sandwiches silly. I cozied up in the driver's seat, engaged the key, and then silence! Nothing! Oh no, now what would I do? No form of telecommunication to alert the boss of my delay. Let's try door number 2. Engage key and click-click. Dead battery. I was late for that special plate. On to door number 3. I jumped into the seat and engaged the key... Spit, sputter, and run, please? It didn't sound healthy. I pushed car number 1 up to car number 3, and let's do the "pass the spark along." Thank you, Jesus—it ran! I turned the key off on number 3. I detached the links between 1 and 3.

I hurried before it died again. Only four miles; I should make it. On the road again—one mile, and all seemed well... Two miles, and I was halfway there. Three miles and I was almost there. Four miles, and it was time to go to work, but what's that? Oh no, no...

no…not that. No power. I was off the road again. I popped the hood and checked it out. I opened it up and said, "Ah!" It was a loosened battery terminal cable. I reattached it and was on my way again until the next time. Thirty minutes later, I was slapping those slices together, but now back on track until the next breakdown. The reward of owning an older, paid-in-cash-for automobile was just like in my life—sometimes my heavenly Father needed to reattach my *battery cable*. The old devil unhooked me through his distractions and temptations from my source of power, Jesus Christ. I got side-lined off road, but praise God I could get charged up and back on the right track through You, Jesus. On the road again—not on my own again—You and me, Jesus, traveling down the road of life together. I couldn't make it on my own; I needed you, Jesus.

Freedom Lost

I will not forget the feeling that came over me that day as the doors locked behind me, and I found myself sharing a room with several other women. The first night, I slept on the top bunk with one blanket. The second night, it was on a cement floor in a plastic sled with one blanket. I had eyes on me with each step I took. The open-door policy in the shower and restroom didn't comfort me either. The freedom I had once enjoyed now eluded me. I had made choices that had left me without certain freedoms. I couldn't just go for a walk, decide what I wanted to cook for dinner, or even decide to watch a program on television. The judge had stated he wanted to make an example of me just days before in his courtroom, and now I was seeing what my choice had cost me. Although I was seeing the consequences of my choices, I was also seeing God's love and mercy for me.

You see, I was facing a felony charge and looking at a prison term of fifteen years, but because I decided to do the right thing and let God have His way in my life, that same judge, who had wanted to make an example of me, was now giving me grace and sentenced me to three days in the local jail. It took much longer for me to make amends to those people my choices had hurt. It took me even longer to forgive myself. With God's help, I was able to pay my debts and make the appropriate amends. I thank Jesus for His love and mercy.

Lung Cancer

In February 2007, during a trip to the doctor's office for what I thought was simply bronchitis, X-ray spotted something in my lungs that looked suspicious. I went through a CT scan and further testing. In March 2007, the news came that it appeared to be lung cancer. The doctor told me that I would need further tests, including MRI and PET scans, and then I would see a specialist. In July 2007, I underwent a biopsy surgery which required taking samples of the spots in my lungs. From there, I saw the pulmonary specialist. He sat me down and said, "Good news…it's not cancer! Bad news, it's a rare lung disease—sarcoidosis. There is no cure. It's progressive and mimics lung cancer." When future growths appeared, it would mean more tests to determine if it was cancer or sarcoidosis. The diagnosis? Steroids, to which I quickly said no. The options? Go to the mountains and dry air with less humidity.

Two weeks later, driving a thirty-four-foot motorhome, I was on my way to Alpine, Wyoming, better known as Star Valley. I was packed with my little black Pomeranian and all the personal stuff one could fit into such a moving home. My husband at that time had started a job two weeks previously out there in Jackson Hole. We lived in an RV park there in Alpine and began a new life, getting to meet new people. We started volunteering at the local animal humane shelter, and eventually, we were invited to a local church there as well. We moved back to Michigan in 2011, but when I fell out of remission, I needed to move back out to Wyoming, and this time I would be going alone (2013). God was with me as I traveled back to Star Valley and started my life without a spouse. I started attending a church closer to where I was living. It was a small church that met in a log cabin. God blessed me as I could look out of my windows onto those beautiful mountains, as I was two blocks from the mountains. In a short time, my health improved, and I was back in remission again.

Perseverance

It was March 3, 2009, when I received a phone call. It announced the tragic and unexpected death of my son-in-law, who had perished while trapped in a fire in his friend's home. He was thirty years old and probably thought he would live a long life. He had two beautiful little daughters who now would grow up without their daddy. The day before he passed away, he had another tattoo added to his many others. This one read "Perseverance" because he wanted it to remind him that he needed to keep trying if he wanted to succeed in life. He had stated that he wanted to become a better father to his daughters. From the world's view, he was a deadbeat dad, but to his girls, he was their daddy no matter what! He struggled in school, faced challenges trying to keep jobs, and had battles with drugs and alcohol. He had been in and out of jail, and one more time would have labeled him a *habitual offender*. He was an angry young man and had sometimes been known to beat my daughter, his then wife. When I heard this, I was reminded of how each of us needs to persevere. Living our lives for the Lord is not promised to be easy, but God will walk with us through our journeys.

Paul often spoke about his *thorn in the flesh* and how he had to rely on God for strength to overcome challenges in his life. While I wasn't certain that my son-in-law had decided to accept Jesus as his Savior, I knew that God had been trying to reach him. When I first met him, he made no bones about being an atheist, but over time, God was using his daughters to teach him about a loving God. My granddaughters had attended a Christian school and church after their parents divorced. They often told their daddy about the Bible stories from their lessons in school.

Last fall, it became difficult for my daughter to enroll the girls in this private school, so she registered them in a public school. He noticed a change in his daughters. He told his family he wanted the girls to return to the private Christian school as soon as he could help with tuition. He admitted that he had come to realize there was indeed a God of the universe. It is my hope and prayer that in his last moments, he reached out to God for salvation. I hope he persevered even in those final moments to make positive changes in his life. That is what God wants for all of us: to keep on keeping on for Him, doing what is necessary to get it right, trying again and again, and getting up when we fall down.

> I press toward the mark for the prize of the
> high calling of God in Christ Jesus. (Philippians
> 3:14)

God wants each of us not to give up, no matter what we might be going through. My son-in-law was found lying beneath his bedroom window when the smoke overtook him. He did not want to give up, even in his final moments. Some of us are struggling with disease or addictions, like alcoholism, yet God tells us to keep pushing through—do not quit!

While I am saddened that my son-in-law is no longer there for his daughters, I am grateful that God is there for them. God is walking alongside them in their sorrow and is carrying them through their tears as well. I read in John 14 how God is not going to leave us without a comforter. Even in sorrow, God comforts my granddaughters, and yes, even my daughter because at one point in her life, she had seen something in him that she was willing to love him for, and as a result, God blessed them with their two beautiful daughters.

None of us knows the hour or the day when our lives will end. On March 11, my twenty-three-year-old grandniece was called home to her loving Lord and Savior. She was so full of life. She had recently found out she had a brain tumor and would be going into surgery on March 9. The pastor prayed with her before she went into the operating room. She knew she might not come back, but she was ready to meet Jesus if it was her time to go. She went in and then the doctors found out they were not able to remove the entire brain tumor. While in this process, she had a stroke, and the family took her off life support two days later. She had been close to my daughter in their younger days. She had often been the one her friends went to for counsel. One of her famous sayings was, "Build a bridge and get over it." The pastor told us at her funeral that she had started building her bridge to Jesus many years before and completed it when she was ushered into His presence on that day. She did not give up building her relationship with the heavenly Father. She also built strong family bridges as well. She was the only granddaughter of my sister-in-law. She was truly special in her own right, yet God saw her even more special when He called her back to Himself. She didn't stop living her life for the Lord, and she kept trying to encourage all those around her to also live for Jesus.

Two funerals in ten days—very different and yet similar in that I saw a lesson from the Lord in them both. Sadness is all around us, and sometimes we think it will pass us by, but it doesn't! God taught me to continue to rely on Him for my strength even in the midst of these sorrows because he loves me so very much that He will go through all this with me.

Webster's definition of perseverance is being able and willing to keep going, continue, or the action of preserving, or steadfast.

> Therefore, my beloved brethren, be ye steadfast, unmovable, always abounding in the work of the Lord. (1 Corinthians 15:58)

> Go ye, therefore, and teach all nations… and lo I am with you always, even unto the end of the age. (Matthew 28:19–20)

God desires us to keep on going even amidst the struggles, and He will be right there with us and yes, even carrying us sometimes. Psalm 23 tells us that even in the shadow of the valley of death, God is with us. I know that truly He is with me and my family through our sadness and tears.

When my daughter collapsed after watching her former mother-in-law do the same, God was there to help me hold my daughter up as well. There in that moment was my daughter, her two little girls, and God holding us and telling us that it would be okay, and we would get up and go on even in our tears. If I can say anything to you who may be reading this today, know that *you are not alone*! God will help you to push through your disease, your pain, your tears, or whatever your struggles may be. God loves each of us so very much.

I will continue to praise Jesus and give Him thanks for the breath He grants me. I will push ahead to share His great love for me and others whom He sent Jesus to die on the cross for all our sins. Even Jesus pushed Himself through to the cross. In the garden, He prayed that if it would be the Father's will to take this from Him to do just that, but He already knew that He was to get up and continue down that road to Calvary. Why? For *you* and *me*, to take upon Himself our sins. Because God loves us so much. Let us keep keeping on for Jesus. Let us not let another moment get by that we are not trying to do all that the Lord would have each of us to do. Some are called to sow the seeds, some to root out the weeds, some of us are to water the sown seeds, while others are to gather the harvest, but whatever each of us is called to do, let us run that race toward the prize of high calling in Christ Jesus.

Amid this sadness, God answered prayers… Someone stepped up to pay the tuition for my granddaughters' education. God gave us blessings even amid this sorrow.

The Phone Call

It was at that moment when I heard the person on the other end of the phone say, "We need your help," that my heart melted away. One moment I was enjoying the beauty of the great Rockies all around me, filled with all its nature, and in the next, I was answering the call to go a thousand miles away to help my family. The hardest thing a mother had to hear was, "I am in trouble, and I need help. Can you come?" There was nothing to consider. I knew where I needed to go, yet getting there wasn't going to be easy. It began with clearing out my apartment, downsizing to what I could fit into my car, and having to say goodbye again to life in the mountains of Star Valley. This was not going to be an easy thing to do by any means.

Just as when I had left my home in the Midwest years before, I cried having to leave my home in the valley. I had to take one last view before I began the three-day drive back to Michigan. I watched as Mother Nature was just starting to prepare for spring. The tops of the mountains were still snow-covered as the animals began to wake up from their winter's nap. I knew I was about to embark on another journey, one I hadn't traveled before—dealing with a loved one who had succumbed to drug addiction. The hardest part was realizing I could not fix the problem for my loved one. I had to simply be there when they hit rock bottom and then be willing to help them grab their rope to pull themselves out of their pit. This was not going to be an easy journey. I cried many tears, spoke many prayers, and sometimes endured being screamed at, yet I had to believe they would find their way out.

After a few years of watching them struggle with drug and alcohol addictions, losing their home, and even their children for a time, and seeing them at their worst, I realized how much I could not fix it. I could only tell them I loved them and that I was there for them. With time, love, and relocating out of state, I was happy to report they had found their way out. It was not easy by any means, as their children suffered just as much in this and even more so because they couldn't understand. I was a mother and grandmother, and I struggled to understand the effects and challenges of addiction. How could I think the children could understand it? Hope was found amid this too. I joined a local support group for families with loved ones trapped in addictions and their cycle. I began to learn so much from their experiences. I wasn't alone. God walked this road with me, so I knew He would grant me strength on this journey.

Now, in 2023, as I put this book together, I am saddened to say that one of my loved ones, who struggled with his addiction, fell back into some of its lures, and as a result, he ended all relationships with me and his son.

A Lost Grandchild

I remember August 8, 2014, as one day I will never forget. The life God gave to you, even if just for a few weeks on this earth, will not be forgotten. The pain you must have endured this day. Today, wee little one, as you return to the Father and your creator, know how much I love you. Grandma loves you so much and is crying tears over you. I am sorry I wasn't given a chance to meet you, but one day, I will see you and your sweet face. I know that words cannot express just how much my heart hurts today. I wish only love for you, wee little one. From today forward, you will forever be in the arms of love. I am sorry, you had to go through this horrible thing today. My wee little one, know Grandma holds you in her heart until that precious time we will meet again—face to face. So, remember this day for the love I hold for you—not the incredible pain—because, wee little one, Grandma loves you oh so much! I thank my Lord Jesus that He loves His children so much and that it is not His desire that any of them feel hurt or pain. Abortion is tears in the eyes of our Father as well as in this grandmother's eyes.

Living in a Camper

My journey began with our move to Wyoming in 2007 but would really begin a new journey for me in 2015 as I found peace in the pines in Georgia. In November of 2015, I came to this peaceful place, unknowingly by God's leading. I had been planning to go somewhere else when suddenly plans would change. I went to the Internet and discovered this campground. I was an emotional wreck inside that only God truly knew.

At first, I stayed away from people, but then God's nature around me began to speak to me. It is often said that nature has such a healing. Well, it was true for me. As I would walk around listening to the birds sing their praises to God and see all the squirrels jumping from tree to tree gathering the pinecones, I began to sense a feeling of peace that I was looking for. I felt the breeze on my face as I walked around the pond. I felt so refreshed as God sent the sunshine upon my face. I saw the blue sky as I looked up in the daylight, and at night, I saw the amazing stars. It was as if God was reaching down to remind me that He was looking out for me.

I began to volunteer helping outside around the campground picking up pine cones and raking up the pine straw. I soon began to see just how much God was going to be answering the desires of my heart, to be a part of a family. You see my biological family had disowned me many years before, and I wanted so much to feel the love of a family. God began to bring healing into my life through a process of time and friendships. I am so grateful for His provision over my life and for His leading me to this place.

Through the years I have come to see this as *home* and find such peace and joy in being here. I started out here as a *snowbird* coming and going with winter but eventually began living here year-round. I left for a while to help out my family in 2020 but returned home in September 2021. God allows me to be among His creation, be a part of a local church, and find opportunities to serve Him. God is so good to me, and I cannot give Him enough praise.

God has carried me through hurricanes and storms both in nature and even in my personal life. Proverbs 3:5–6 is my life verse:

> Trust in the Lord with all thin heart and lean not unto thine own understanding. In all thy ways acknowledge Him and He shall direct thy path.

When I walked around the water in the pond, I saw the beautiful hues of blue and green, which was just so cleansing. Even the fish popped up from the water as I sang His praises. The doves stopped to coo and offer up their praises as well. The cardinals flew around to show me that God is an ever-present presence in my life. If I have any stress, I find that it leaves me as I walk just as the dew rises up from the grass when the sun rises. There is sweetness in the aroma of the trees and bushes in this place.

Learning Joy

It was December 2021, and I was asking God for the word for me for the coming year He spoke to me about true joy. "The joy of the Lord is my strength" (Nehemiah 8:10). Little did I know in that moment what lessons I would soon learn as the New Year approached. God was showing me how to focus on positive things as opposed to negative things. He wanted me to find joy where others may have been seeing a negative thing. So would my journey begin.

I needed to purchase a camper to live in as the cabin I had been staying in was in need of being remodeled. I looked up on the Internet and found one yet God soon closed the door to it as the owner changed their mind. I was convinced the owner was going to change his mind again as the camper was everything I was hoping for. Well, God wanted to teach me about joy. I did find a camper and went to check it out. My first mistake? I didn't ask anyone with experience in campers to go along with me. My second mistake was thinking that it was within my budget so it must be the one. My third mistake? I hadn't taken the time to seek God about this camper and simply told the man that I would take it. I gave him a deposit and made plans to come back with help to bring it to the campground. The owner mentioned several times that his father had told him often that a man's word is his word and, to be honest. I accepted that he was being truthful with me.

As I looked the camper over, I saw some tiny flaws, yet I was confident I could make this my little home and be happy. So I began my journey, but I soon learned that I had more to learn from my Lord. You see, not long after getting the camper, I found there were many flaws that hadn't been told to me in the beginning. Soon the question was this: did I jump into this decision too quickly on my own? Yes was the answer God showed me yet He reminded me that I had to be joyous and give Him the praise for what He was teaching me.

When the roof began to leak, I praised the Lord, I still had shelter. When the refrigerator quit, I praised Him that I was able to borrow one until I could replace the refrigerator. When the windows began to leak, and the wall needed to be torn out, I praised Him that friends were here to help me replace the wall and show me how to fix it. When I needed to get a propane tank, I was given an exchange tank until I could purchase the bigger one-hundred-pound tank. I was blessed with a friend to climb up on the roof to reseal the roof. I was blessed to find friends willing to help me exchange the old refrigerator and put in the new one. God continued to show me how blessed I was and to let joy flow through me rather than walk around complaining about the problems this camper was presenting.

As I write this, I share that once more, God provided me the blessing of getting a camper that has those things I desired in the beginning. It was through the struggles of the lessons I was learning that I truly could see the joy God was giving me. I had to also learn how to forgive the owner of the camper for his deception because it was what the Father wanted me to do. It wasn't easy yet God walked me through that as well.

As the end of 2022 came, I sought the Lord to seek what words would become my words for 2023. The words He chose for me in 2023 are *strength* and *courage*. Little did I know how much strength or courage I would need in the coming year.

> Have I not commanded thee? Be strong
> and of a good courage; be not afraid, neither be
> thou dismayed; for the Lord thy God is with thee
> whithersoever thou goest. (Joshua 1:9)

God Is My Comfort

I happened to be looking over my Facebook and noticed my niece asking for prayers for her father. I reached out to try and find out exactly what was going on with my brother, her father. To my sadness, I discovered that he was in the hospital miles away and was not doing very well. He had been a cancer survivor previously but was now fighting COVID. It wasn't long before he was placed on a ventilator to help him breathe. Within a short amount of time, my brother passed away just weeks after celebrating his sixty-second birthday. Because I wasn't accepted in the family anymore, I wasn't allowed to travel up to Michigan for the funeral. I will be forever grateful that in June 2020, he and I had spoken to each other, and he knew that I loved him. We hugged that day as I walked out to my car.

You see, my father had refused me any relationship with my siblings, my mother, or himself since 1975, although there had been attempts in 2007 to resolve it. He said I was dead to the family, and he made sure others knew not to reach out to me. That day in June 2020, he refused to even be in the same room with me as he had allowed me to come to visit my mother since COVID was on the rise. My mother and I, with my brother, did share some heartfelt thoughts. When I left, she told me I was welcome to visit again, yet my father saw to it that we had no further communication after that day. So when my brother passed, I was struck with such grief, yet I knew that we had made peace in that meeting just two years before. I learned that day in the meeting with my brother and mother that my father possibly had pancreatic cancer but was refusing any help. On December 1, 2022, he passed away as well, and again, I was not welcome to be a part of that funeral. Just weeks before his passing, I also lost a brother-in-law as his diabetes and stroke claimed him. My sister was struggling with the loss of our brother, her husband, and then our father. I found joy in knowing that even in my heartache over the loss of not being able to be with my biological family, God provided me with a family here at the campground that surrounded me with their love as I grieved. God knew how much I needed them.

My Heartache

I will never forget that day, July 28, 2023, when I heard those hurtful words as you uttered your lies. You stated I was unstable, unreliable, and should not have any part of a relationship with you. No words were ever so hurtful because in my heart I knew that God and truth were right there with me. I watched as you laughed out in the lobby and again your smiles as you walked across the parking lot. Yet what you didn't see were the tears I cried in the car in that parking lot. You are my gift from God, as well as your sibling, and yet your words were like a sword through my heart. Yet amid my hurt and pain, I had to let go and let God become my source of comfort and peace. God loves you even more than I do, as it was He who blessed me with your life when doctors said I wouldn't be able to have or carry children after your brother had passed away. I know that God continues to be there for me despite the deep pain your words and that of your sibling left in my heart that day. It is my desire that one day, you and your siblings will see God's love is even greater than the love I have for all of you.

Recently my pastor has been presenting messages on why hardships come our way. In 1 Peter, verse 7,

> That the trial of your faith, being much more precious than of gold that perisheth, though it be tried with fire, might be found unto

praise and honour and glory at the appearing of
Jesus Christ.

The reason some of us go through hardships is to give praises
to our heavenly Father when we return unto Him. I love my Savior,
Jesus Christ, and will continue to lean on Him in those tough times.

Conclusion

> He who dwelleth in the secret place of the
> Most High shall abide under the shadow of the
> Almighty. (Psalm 91:1)

> Thou art my hiding place. (Psalm 32:7)

When one is alone, they desire a place to be alone because that is what most of them feel and know: being alone. God has promised us that He will be that hiding place for us when we are alone.

> The Lord is the light of my salvation; whom
> shall I fear? The Lord is the strength of my life; of
> whom shall I be afraid? (Psalm 27:1)

Not everyone experiences "being alone" or being lonely. Many have spouses to share their lives with, but what about the widows or the widowers? What about those who aren't in this group but are alone, physically, due to a divorce or a circumstance in their life? Where do they fit in? How many times will a single person find themselves amid a group, where they may feel like they do not belong? Many times, they can be too old to be in a college group, too young to be with a seniors group, and do not feel comfortable in married groups. So where does this person go? Jesus knew what it was to be alone. His disciples couldn't stay awake with Him in the garden to pray. He prayed alone while they were asleep. Jesus took upon Himself the sins of us all, alone. God knew the work His Son, Jesus, would be required to do, alone; no one else could do what He would do for all mankind. God's Word tells me I can go to Jesus for my hiding place, my refuge. He knows what it is to be alone. He knows what it is like to be rejected by others and to be alone. God tells us we don't need to be afraid because He is our strength. If anyone experienced loneliness, it was Jesus as He died on Calvary's cross. He cried out to His Father, "Why hast Thou forsaken Me?"

For those who feel alone, we need to remember there is one who truly knows how we feel. He felt the loneliness as a man while on this earth. Jesus is there for all who feel alone.

> The Lord is my strength and my shield; my
> heart trusted in Him, and I am helped. Therefore,
> my heart greatly rejoiceth, and with my song will
> I praise Him. (Psalm 28:7)

Pressing On

Quite some time ago, I heard a message in Philippians 3:12–14 about pressing on toward the prize of the high calling of God. As we near the latter part of 2023, we can be reminded that God is a God of endings and new beginnings, as well as of second chances. There are many examples in the Bible of those who were given a second chance. An example of one such person was Samson. He lost his eyes because of the Philistines. He lost his strength when Delilah betrayed him to those Philistines. Yet as he ground their wheat, he asked God to grant him strength once more to destroy the enemies that now imprisoned him. When led to the arena to be mocked, he was placed between two pillars where God granted him a second chance. God gave him the strength with which he pulled down the pillars of that arena. Samson killed more in his death than when he lived, all to the glory of God. He pressed on toward the prize of the high calling of his God.

Webster's definition of a resolution is "the act of determining or to make clear or understandable." The prefix *re-* means "back" or "again," while *solutions* comes from the root word *solve*; therefore, we are again to make clear or understandable our goal of pressing on for God.

The prodigal son resolved to go back home again after spending time in the pig pen. He realized that he was loved at home and would press on to his prize—a loving father. His father awaited him with the best robe and a ring and had his servants slaughter and prepare a fatted calf. What a prize for pressing on.

Sometimes it can become very difficult to press on, especially when we are in the midst of the valley or a struggle that is weighing us down. We need to remember, first, God is love, and He loves us! Secondly, we were created for love—both to give it and to receive it. Then thirdly, press on in God's love, up, out, or through that valley.

Satan is the author of confusion. He does not want to see Christians succeed. He doesn't want us to press on; rather, he wants us to just throw in the towel because it is hurting too much. It is helpful to remember if we can stay focused on Jesus; the blessing is just around the corner. Press on. Hold on. Look up. Even if we do fall down and slip, God does grant us second chances and sometimes third, fourth, and fifth.

God never promised us an easy road, just that He would never leave us nor forsake us. He said He would be with us even to the point of carrying us. If I can say anything to encourage you as you read this, I would say the prize at the end of this will be worth it all! Praise the Lord. Heaven awaits those who have chosen Jesus Christ. Let each of us determine to press on toward that prize. Let each of us determine to shine forth as a lighthouse in a darkened place of hurting hearts. There are many who need the healing God offers each of us. God inhabits the praise of His people, so let us praise Him for what He is doing and continue to resolve to press on in our journeys.

Personally, I praise the Lord for the many second chances He has provided to me throughout my life journey. I want my life to become a reflection of God's love. In 2000, I determined that the following year would have my motto, "Shine, don't whine." God has taught me many lessons since that time as well. The enemy hates it when we choose to praise the Lord, especially when we are in the middle of a struggle or in the valley. So join with me as we continue to "press up, press through, press on, press across for the glory of the Cross."

I have been reminded so many times in my life, and throughout it, that I am not on this journey alone. I have suffered abuse, heartache, loss, grief, loneliness, and living with a rare disease, yet in it all, I believe God has given me a purpose. I use my writings and my experiences to encourage each of you who may be reading this: God loves you, too, and you do not have to go through life feeling alone. I have struggled with my own alcohol addiction and with my guilt in the contributing to the ending of my marriage. I have seen God's mercy in action in the middle of a situation that could have given me fifteen years in prison. I am blessed beyond measure by just how much my heavenly Father loves me. It is my desire and prayer that each of you reading this will know you are *not* alone, as God can be with you wherever you may be in your life.

> For God so loved the world that He gave His only begotten Son that whosoever believeth in Him should not perish but have everlasting life. For God sent not His Son into the world to condemn the world; but that the world through Him might be saved. (John 3:16–17)

> A new commandment I give unto you, That ye love one another; as I have loved you, that ye also love one another. (John 13:34)

Acknowledgments

I wish to thank my Lord and Savior for planting this book within my heart. I want to thank those dearest to me who have supported me as I struggled through my life's journeys and even walked in the valleys with me. I want to thank my spiritual family here at Beaver Run, as God gave you to me as a gift of His blessing of what a family is when God is at the forefront of one's life. I owe my faith foundation to the faith of my grandmothers who displayed their love for Jesus in every part of their lives, and I look forward to the day I see you again. I thank the Lord for my home church and the messages my pastor presents each week to help me stay focused on my Lord.

Thank you to all who helped in the printing of this book as well.

> Rejoice always, pray without ceasing, in everything give thanks; for this is the will of God in Christ Jesus for you. (1 Thessalonians 5:16–18)

> And whatsoever ye do, do it heartily, as unto the Lord, and not unto men. (Colossians 3:23)

> For I know the plans I have for you. (Jeremiah 29:11)

About the Author

Tiffany Rose is a simple countrywoman. Her faith and love for God have carried her through her struggles, as well as the joys of living her life. Tiffany enjoys being outdoors around nature. She enjoys writing about her journey called life.